# Forming Jural Assemblies
## *Building Blocks of the Republic*

FIRST EDITION
March 2011

Copyright © 2011
by
David E. Robinson

Attorney General pro tem
for the Maine Republic free state

All Rights Reserved
Parts of this book may be reproduced subject to due and specific acknowledgment of their source.

MAINE-PATRIOT.com
3 Linnell Circle
Brunswick, Maine 04011

maine-patriot.com

*There must be a righteous government for God to Bless the nation.*

# Forming Jural Assemblies

## Contents

Introduction ---------------------------------------------- 7
1. A Biblical Foundation ------------------------------- 9
2. What Is Really Real? ------------------------------- 11
3. Regarding Levels ----------------------------------- 15
4. Two Government Structures ---------------------- 17
5. Representative Government vs Democracy -- 21
6. Republic vs Republican ---------------------------- 23
7. Two Simple Easy Steps ---------------------------- 25
8. The General Assembly & Jural Assemblies --- 31
9. Begin With The General Assembly -------------- 33
10. Duties & Calls To Action -------------------------- 37
11. Forming Jural Assemblies ----------------------- 43
12. Forming de jure Grand Juries ------------------- 45
13. Record Keeping By Whom ----------------------- 47
14. Bureau Of Republic Records -------------------- 49
15. Duties Of The Commissioner -------------------- 51
16. Law Of The Land Or Law Of The Sea --------- 53
17. Historical Note -------------------------------------- 55
18. Sample Constitution ------------------------------- 59
19. Sample Declaration Of Intent -------------------- 63
20. Quick Lesson In Politics -------------------------- 74
21. The Initial Process --------------------------------- 79
22. Ken Cousen's Declaration Of Intent ----------- 83
23. Quick Lesson In The Economy ------------------ 89
   Re: Robert's Rules Of Order --------------------- 95

*Building Blocks of the Republic*     5

# Introduction

We-The-People are the First Level of Government in a Republic.

As one of We-The-People you can see how you, in a Jural Assembly, have Power and Authority "over" your elected free state officials of "state government" through your **State Settlement Constitution.**

Your **State Settlement Constitution** is the road map of authority for your elected free state "Officials" which includes the "process" by which you have the power and the authority to "hire and fire" these "servants."

In your **State Settlement Constitution** you need to make provision for you, the We-The-People, to have the power and authority of removal at any time during an elected official's "term of office" to "take him out of office," via proper notice and another election which will keep the wheels of government from stalling in its track.

You must have a process spelled out and pre-agreed-to in your **State Settlement Constitution**.

Remember, We-The-People will have "delegated" some of our "autonomous power and authority" to "servant representatives" — state and national Congressional people who form the two Congressional bodies of people called the Senate and the House of Representatives in their free states.

We delegate some of our authority to the above mentioned servants via the **State Settlement Constitution** and **Constitution for the united States of America.** (uSA)

**Why do we do this?**
We do this because there are certain matters that one man or woman cannot deal with on a personal-vote issue.

So there are "delegated" powers to other men and women who we permit to make decisions for us by "representing" us.

**Representative government** stems from God's Old Testament instruction to have one man represent a body of 10 men, then from those 10 men, one representative is chosen to represent 100 men, then from those 100 men, one representative is chosen to represent 1000 men, and on and on.

# 1
# A Biblical Foundation

You are most likely aware that in the formation of the government the Founders decided to utilize three separate and distinct branches: **Judicial, Legislative** and **Executive**.

But do you know what influenced that decision? It was **Isaiah 33:22** which reads:

*"For the Lord is our Judge, our Lawgiver, and our King ; he will save us."*

The Lord is our **Judge**, this is the *Judicial* side.
The Lord is our **Lawgiver**, this is the *Legislative* side.
The Lord is our **King**, this is the *Executive* side.

The concept was that if God was to save and protect this nation then he must be over all three branches of government.

This is what it means to be *"One Nation, under God."*

*"In the government of this Commonwealth, the legislative department shall never exercise the executive and judicial powers, or either of them; the executive shall never exercise the legislative or judicial powers, or either of them; the judicial shall never exercise the legislative and executive powers, or either of them; to the end that it may be "government of laws and not of men."*

(Constitution of the Commonwealth of Mass. 1780 A.D.).

Daniel Webster said, *"Education is useless without the Bible".*

George Washington said, *"It is the duty of all nations to acknowledge the providence of Almighty God, to obey His will, to be grateful for His benefits, and humbly to implore His protection and favor".*

James Madison said, *"We have staked the whole future of our new nation, not upon the power of government; far from it. We have staked the future of all our political constitutions upon the capacity of each of ourselves to govern ourselves according to the moral principles of the Ten Commandments".*

Patrick Henry said, *"It cannot be emphasized too strongly or too often that this great Nation was founded not by religionists, but by Christians; not on religions, but on the Gospel of Jesus Christ".*

Many years ago a Frenchman, Alexis de Tocqueville, came to observe this country. After doing so, he noted that our independence was based upon our dependence upon God. And he warned that if this nation ever loses its dependence on God that it would lose its independence.

*"O Lord, revive your work in the midst of the years."* (Habakkuk 3:2.)

## 2
# What Is Really Real?

**Today our society - all of it - is based on a fiction.**

Fictitious plaintiffs (UNITED STATES) versus fictitious defendants (JOHN DOE) in fictitious courts with *non-consensual* fictitious laws (statutes). Fictitious contracts (DEEDS OF TRUST) are made by fictitious parties, granting fictitious property (TITLES and LEGAL DESCRIPTIONS) to other fictitious parties.

You may say, "I want only the *real thing* or something that is *real.*"

**Real:** a *'thing'* (*same root as* **Republic**); actually being or existing; not fictitious or imaginary; genuine; not artificial, counterfeit or fictitious; not affected; not assumed.

But what is *real?* Is matter or even your body real? — Or are they a composite of thought particles and sound waves with agreed upon electromagnetic energies that vibrate in fluctuating patterns so as to reflect light, thus giving the illusion of varying degrees of solidity, light, color and motion? Whew!

Let's go to the MATRIX where Morpheus introduced Neo to the *"construct."*
**Morpheus:** "Your appearance is what we call *'residual self image'* — the mental projection of your digital self."

**Neo** asks: Is this real?

Building Blocks of the Republic

**Morpheus:** "What is real? How do you define real? If you are talking about what you can feel, what you can taste, what you can see, then real is simply electrical signals interpreted by your mind."

Does this idea sound familiar? Have you ever heard of this concept before?

Genesis 1:26: *"And God said, Let us make man in our image, after our likeness:"*

**Man:** Adam - of the earth, hypocrite. Image: a phantom, illusion, resemblance, a representative figure, an idol, a vain show, to shade.

How is it, that by saying you are a "man," you are being a hypocrite?

**Hypocrite:** a player of a part on the stage; simulation, to feign; to separate and put under; the act or practice of simulating or feigning to be what one is not; especially the assuming of a false appearance.

Is it possible that we have been looking at God and man from the wrong prospective, looking *AT* God, instead of looking *TO God?*

Are you *"of the earth; earthly"* — a creation, an illusion, a representative figure? Is the body real or is it an "image," a vain show, a reflection of what is in the mind?

**Morpheus:** "The world exists as a *'neural interactive simulation'* — you've been living in a *dream-world* Neo!"

When Neo was in the "jump program" where he was going to jump across to the other skyscraper, he let doubt overcome him and he fell. Afterwards he was in pain and commented to Morpheus, "I thought it wasn't real?"

**Morpheus:** "Your mind *makes* it real — your body cannot live without the mind."

**Neo:** "Wait a minute! If there really is nothing real — then what really *is* real? *Really!*

**Morpheus:** "Well, you know *you* are real don't you? — not your body — just *you?* Once you have that stable datum, then you can create reality with your mind. Not by trying or wishing or hoping or thinking or even believing something into existence — these words are way too wimpy. One must create reality by **KNOWING!**

Remember what Morpheus said to Neo when they were sparring in the training construct? He asked Neo, "How did I beat you? Do you think my being faster or stronger has anything to do with my muscles in this place? Do you think that it is air you are breathing? What are you waiting for? You are *faster* than this! Don't *THINK* you are, *KNOW YOU ARE!* Come on, stop *TRYING* to hit me, and **HIT** me!"

What is reality?

Can one have reality without *'agreement'?* If two people were playing chess, then one could say they were playing a "game of chess" — a reality. But, what if *one* of them said **"I am not playing this game anymore,"** would there be a reality to the two people of "a game of chess"? or not. What if one started playing on the same board with the same pieces with the same player, *but he changed the rules to* "checkers"?! Wow, would that ever cause some confusion with the guy playing under *chess* rules!

**We all can do this!**

*Building Blocks of the Republic*

We can change the rules and continue to play where we are right now in the same environment (board) with the same people (pieces). By our word, *we can make our own rules* and state, **"this is how the game will be played. From now on we play by MY rules!"**

**Word:** Greek *logos*; something said including the thought, topic, reasoning, motive; a computation; expression; from *lego* - to lay forth; relate in words; to show or make known one's thoughts.

**Flesh:** flesh, stripped of the skin; meat; body - a symbol of what is *external* as opposed to the *mind or spirit* - human being; from *sairo* — to brush off; to sweep away.

John 1:1: **"In the beginning was the Word, and the Word was with God, and the Word was God. All things were made by him; and without him was not anything made that was made."**

Our world has been waiting for us to tell it what to do, all along. It will do *anything* we command it to do.

It will do anything we command it to do — if we only could figure out *WHAT* we want it to do. **Decide,** take responsibility for the consequences, **destroy fear and doubt, 'command'** what you envision and attain it — *success.* Then, *V'wa-la!* — completion! Make your Word manifest itself in the physical realm.

John 1: 14: **"The Word was made flesh."**

**We-The-People are the First Level of Government in the Republic!**

# 3
# Regarding Levels

We have been mis-taught that the "levels" of government are "top down" from the federal, state, and local levels. And we've been mis-taught that the "branches" of government are the Executive, the Legislative and the Judicial.

We need to now re-program the American mind with a new/old concept of "levels" because we need to understand the "power and authority" that we have as We-The-People OVER the elected and appointed "public servants", via elections and the State and County Settlement Constitutions under which we work.

In the new/old order of the re-inhabited Republic all the men and women who hold elected, appointed, and volunteer positions of "government" — for whatever period of time — are always a part of their Jural Assembly, whether at the state or county level.

They have a "Voice and Vote" in the We-The-People Jural Assembly while they hold their specific "government" position on their one de jure Grand Jury.

We-The-People, in Jural Assembly, are the governmental authority on this land. We-The-People, in Jural Assembly, are the employer of everyone working in and for the government. They are our servants, i.e. our employees.

**We-The-People** are the 1st Level of Government.
**The Legislature** is the 2nd . . .
**The Executive** is the 3rd . . .
**The Judicial** is the 4th . . .

This order of Levels comes from the Constitution for the United states of America. Check it out.

The Preamble comes first, with We-The-People. The article "The" in We-The-People is capitalized here for prominence, and its title is "the Constitution for the United States of America.

The **Legislature** is defined in Article I.
The **Executive** is defined in Article II.
The **Judicial** is defined in Article III.

There is a reason for this order:

**Article I** - defines who the creator of policy is; who has the authority to create and pass bills of law;

**Article II** - defines who has the authority to sign the bills into law; and execute them.

**Article III** - defines who, if challenged, has the authority to determine whether a law is Constitutional or not — and even whether or not the law is righteous and a good thing for We-The-People.

The Grand Jury is part of the Judicial. And we find the lower case "united States" in the Declaration of Independence.

# 4
# Two Government Structures

**Bottom up Government:**

We-The-People form the 1st level of government by Assembly and provide documents for the 2nd level, the County, - and the 3rd level, the State, - and the 4th level, the Nation.

We use the adjective "national" to differentiate from the adjective "federal" which is associated with the de facto, i.e. false, fabricated, fake, government that exists in fact today here in America. There might also be other local Assemblies "within" the We-The-People county structure, such as Township, Parish, City, etc.

**To summarize:**

The two basic structures or "levels" of government within the Constitutional Republic for the United states of America are . . .

| are . . . | The other one is . . . |
|---|---|
| 1. **We-The-People** | 1. **We-The-People** |
| 2. **The Legislature** | 2. **County** |
| 3. **The Executive** | 3. **State** |
| 4. **The Judicial** | 4. **Nation** |

**We-The-People** are not a branch of government but when we do speak about the Branches of government, it is "within the framework" of We-The-People who make up the Jural Assembly remembering that the We-The-People Jural Assembly is the creator of those branches.

We-The-People in Jural Assembly hold the power "over the Branches" of our government.

*Building Blocks of the Republic*

The Branches are the **Legislative, Executive,** and **Judicial** branches which include the de jure Grand Juries and the Courts.

When these concepts are accepted by everyone, they should go into all future textbooks regarding the "government" of this country. We also need to separate the subjects once again into the foundational areas of **history, civics, government, ethics, math,** etc.

As learning the sound of the letters before hooking them together, so it should be for subject matter, before we mush them all together as in the current system of teaching.

Today everything is mushed together right from the start by "association" and being "inter-related" without teaching the separate components first. No wonder there is confusion so students can't see or understand the specifics.

But first we need to sever the International Agreements* signed by President Bush, Sr., and Clinton which put our education system under the UN's UNESCO, which has already written a third of all textbooks, by 2005.

What's horrific about this is that the "content" of these textbooks promotes the UN's Earth Charter under the misleading term "sustainable development" which is . . .

1. **Earth worship** (pantheism);
2. **Evolution;**
3. **Socialized medicine;**
4. **World federalism;**
5. **Animal Rights;**
6. **Income redistribution;**
7. **Contraception;**
8. **World-wide education including "spiritual education";**

9. **Adoption of the gay-rights agenda;**
10. **Elimination of nuclear weapons and the right to bear arms,** and 5 other untoward positions.

The UN's Earth Charter is a broad religious, ideological and political agenda used in public schools to change the values and morals of our children. Already one generation of children has gone through this mind-altering, controlling, brainwashing, and programming/reprogramming, to eradicate every last thought of the God in whom we trust!

\*Presidents have no authority to sign "agreements," only treaties ratified by Congressional approval, but FDR started this with the Yalta Agreement in order to by-pass any Congressional "oversight", and yet today, hundreds/thousands of "signed international agreements" have been signed by Presidents and their reps which come to have the same "force and effect of law" as do *actual* treaties! This has been a great injustice on We-The-People.

*Building Blocks of the Republic*

# 5
# Representative Government versus Democracy

We have been programmed to believe that we have "a representative government" via what is called a "democratic republic." A "democratic republic" is the "powers that be" trying to keep us placated so they can continue to spin their power and control over our lives.

A democracy is socialism. It is government by majority rule where 51% get their way while 49% do not. Democracy is a "here-today-gone-tomorrow" whim of society. It is NOT a Republican Form of government. (These words are in Article IV, Section 4, of our National Constitution.)

What we have now instituted are de jure Grand Juries. If a bad law is passed, the Grand Jury can stop it from being implemented and declare it null and void, because unconstitutional, and cast it out.

Through the Jural Assemblies we have the means of having elections according to our State Settlement Constitution. The people can fire and hire their elected representative when they don't follow the people's will.

Jural Assemblies could institute something like a "3-strikes-and-you're-out" plan for their elected officials.

Strike 1. If one bad law is introduced and passed by the Legislature, the Grand Jury would give We-The-People Notice of the writer of the bill and which Legislators voted for it.

Strike 2. With the second occurrence, it's a Notice in the same fashion.

Strike 3. The third time that the Grand Jury needs to process a bad, unconstitutional law or bill from that Legislator, it could implement an election per its "fire and hire" authority according to the State Settlement Constitution, for one, several, or all of the Legislature in existence at that time.

No longer will We-The-People sit idly by an watch "elected servant" have a hey-day with incessant, insane, oppressive control over our lives. There are enough of us throughout the 50 states who have banded together for our protection and who have pledged our lives, our fortunes, and our sacred honor to each other to re-inhabit the Republic.

We will not allow defeat. It's not on our list. We are giving the Republic our all. Amen.

# 6
# Republic vs Republican

**Know the difference between these two words!**

The use of the adjective, "Republican," is not necessarily the opposite of the adjective, "Democratic."

When we use the phrase **"Republican Form of Government"** (meaning Republic-type) it is in reference to the Constitution; it has nothing to do with the two political parties everyone is accustomed to.

"Republic" is a noun; and "Republican" is an adjective.

Many writers in the past incorrectly used the noun "republic" when the adjective "republican" was needed instead. This was to emphasize the position of the "Republic" we've re-inhabited vs anyone incorrectly believing that we're referring to the de facto "republican" party or the de facto government, or other elected officials, etc.

We do not want anyone who is currently "democratic" thinking that we are favoring the Republicans of the commonly-known Republican Party, or that we're siding with the Republicans of that Party, or that we are "anti" the Democrats or their Party.

We will always state **"Republican Form of Government"** with the three main words capitalized, as they are in the national Constitution (Article IV, Section 4).

A republican state is not a Republic; it's a **Republican free state,** or a free state of the Republic instead.

*Building Blocks of the Republic*

# 7
# One or Two easy Steps

For a Man or Woman, over the age of 18, to become part of the **General Assembly for [your; the Maine?] free State** of the Republic for the united States of America, the following documents are shown in the order in which they are used to create the structural **Republican Form of Government**.

### THE FIRST STEP:

Declare your independence from the corporate world by autographing (*signing with your autograph*) your personal:

### Declaration of Sovereign Rights
*held by Indigenous Power*

**Indigenous Power** is your innate, inborn, native, natural power and authority over your life, as a blessed and favored, holy spirit directed and guided son or daughter of God.

The autographing of this *"document of release" from the confusions of the foreign Babylonish world,* makes you a **"denizen"** (*an inhabitant on the land*) of the **re-inhabited Republic for the united States of America** (uSA).

Your **DSR** (*Declaration of Sovereign Rights*) **is stated in the following words** . . .

"**In the Beginning Almighty God** created all men equal; that they are created with Sovereign Rights held by Indigenous Power and endowed by their Creator with certain unalienable Rights. A free state is established when one people join together in a common unity to secure their natural God-given rights and sovereignty. To secure their sovereignty and right to life, liberty, and the pursuit of happiness, governments are instituted among men, deriving their just powers from the consent of the governed; to be exercised by elected officials as surrogate power for the free state.

"When surrogate power officials assume the rights of sovereign Indigenous Power as supreme; a free state inverts into a state which usurps the sovereignty of the people and they become mere subjects of mandatory conformity, victims of suppression of natural rights and tyranny. Corrupted surrogate power has no indigenous authority of its own, therefore, I declare by Almighty God in peaceable One People Assembly" [the following Covenant Affirmation] . . .

"**I am** created equal to all men with Sovereign Rights held by Indigenous Power. I solemnly affirm, publish and declare;

"**I am** local to <u>name here the state your are lawfully settled in</u> free state Settlement; lawfully settled in <u>name here your county settlement</u> County Settlement and in Order to form a more perfect free state, establish Justice, insure domestic Tranquility, provide for the common Defence, promote the general Welfare, and secure the Blessings of Liberty for our Posterity and free state; I consent to uphold and keep the Peace or delegate power of Sovereign Rights held by Indigenous Power by county and free state Settlement Constitution for the lawful Protections, Freedoms, and Rights of the sovereign people in these free and independent United states of America. In support to this Declaration, with a firm reliance on Divine Providence we mutually pledge our lives, our fortunes and our sacred honor. By autograph signature under Witness Protection my Declaration of Sovereign Rights held by Indigenous Power is supreme."


**The above Declaration is a Covenant.**
A Covenant is a formal, solemn, binding agreement, usually under seal, between 2 or more parties especially for the performance of some action; it is also a common law action to recover damages for breach of a contract such as the Constitution for the united States of America (uSA).

This autographed (*signed*) Covenant will be witnessed by the autographs (*signatures*) of 2 Witnesses, and delivered to the **Governor** of the American free state Assembly now existing in your state, for his official **Seal** and for the Assembly Records which will be protected and maintained in the official records of the new world order of the re-inhabited **Republic for the united States of America** (uSA).

You'll be a part of the **General Assembly for [your] free State** upon completing this Declaration. In the General Assembly you do not have a "Voice and Vote" in the Jural Assembly business meetings, you cannot participate in holding positions and offices, and you cannot be on the de jure Grand Juries, but you will be able to witness "open" Jural Assembly meetings and know that you have taken the first step of separating yourself from the existing, de facto corporation masquerading as a government.

## THE SECOND STEP:

In addition to now being a denizen member of the **General Assembly for [your] free State of the re-inhabited Republic of the uSA,** you may *choose* to be a **Jurist** and participate actively in the **Jural Assemblies** of your state and county locale.

Any man or woman over the age of 18 who has become part of the **General Assembly for [your] free State** can become part of the **Jural Assemblies** of your state and county locale . . .

By *signing with your autograph* your personal:

### Jural Covenant of Office

**Jural:** of and relating to law; of and relating to rights and obligations.

**A Jurist** is one who knows, engages in, and will uphold matters of law. A qualified Jurist may be called, elected or appointed to serve in positions of delegated authority in the free state of the **Republic for the united States of America (uSA).** Jurists may be called upon to serve on a **Jury Panel** as a Juror on a Grand Jury, Trial Jury, Special Jury, Jural Assembly, or remain collected in a Jury pool for reserves as alternates, or on select committees, as select office holders, or be actually seated upon one of the many Juries that shall exist from the county lever on up.

### Jural Covenant of Office

The Jural Covenant of Office is a declaration in which you will swear to or affirm the following . . .

"I declare my Sovereign Rights are held by Indigenous Power. In One People Assembly in this free state, with a firm reliance on Divine Providence, I will support, protect and defend Almighty Freedom, and the Natural God-given Rights and Privileges of the sovereign people of this free state. I am sentient and of FREE Will, and by this covenant I agree to accept and serve my duty to perform as a Jurist serving local to <u>the free state you are lawfully settled in</u>."

You will solemnly swear to or affirm by Jural covenant local to <u>the county you are lawfully settled in county settlement</u> county settlement; lawfully settled within the geographical boundary of <u>the free state you are living in</u> free state Settlement . . .

"I will delegate power from Sovereign Rights held by Indigenous Power. If appointed or elected to any office serving the people in the free state or **Republic for the united States of America** (uSA) and I accept such calling. I will faithfully serve this office. I will uphold, support, preserve, protect and defend my local **county Settlement Constitution, free state Settlement Constitution, Declaration of Independence**, July 4, 1776 and **Republic for the united States of America Constitution** 1789 and c.1791. I will perform and fulfill all Jural duties and administer the laws of this free state and the **Republic for the united States of America** (uSA) with respect to its people faithfully, impartially, peacefully, honorably, and never contrary to the Law of Almighty God. Representing no one through envy, hatred, malice, covetousness, or ill-will, and leaving no one unrepresented because of fear, favor, affection, reward or enticements. Investigating without restraint all matters of knowledge which have been brought forth unto me in such impartial capacity, keeping all such counsel and deliberations at all times secret for protection of the People. I solemnly affirm to do all of this to the best of my ability and understanding as a sacred covenant between men and the sovereign people I am about to serve, local to these free and independent **united States of America** and the **Republic for which it stands** and the **Almighty Creator**, so help me God."

"May Heaven and Earth be One Eternal Witness this day, Affirmed and autographed by signature **in Grace centered in Almighty God** by me."

You now qualify to be an active participant in the **Grand Jury** due processes of law. **The Grand Jury** is the "engine of the train" to absolute earthly freedom under God.

**The Jural Assembly** is comprised of men and woman, over the age of 25, who are learning to be self-governed responsible Citizens, who hold Power and Authority, and have a "voice and vote" in the world, and who can Hire and Fire, in Jural Assembly, the elected representatives they choose to represent them in their free state.

# 8
# The General Assembly & Jural Assemblies

**Everyone** who comes into the Republic becomes part of the **General Assembly for [your] free State:**

Everyone who autographs his or her **Declaration of Sovereign Rights held by Indigenous Power** is part of the **General Assembly for [your] free State**.

Picture a huge auditorium with a balcony inside the main room. Everyone is seated there. You are in the position of watching and listening, and witnessing, but you cannot participate in the business of the Jural Assembly meeting being held on the floor below. You have no vote in the business of the free state Republican Form of Government.

**JURAL ASSEMBLIES:**

If you autographed the **Jural Covenant** as well, you become part of the Jural Assembly of the state. These are the people within the General Assembly who have a "voice and vote". They will vote on all the decisions of the free state's business. Also, these are the men and women who can hold positions and offices within the free state, whether by volunteering, being appointed or elected, and then approved by the Jural Assembly.

The word "jural" does not mean being on a "jury." So in our "auditorium picture", the jural people have left the balcony, by autographing a **Jural Covenant,** and have moved to the Floor of the hall where jural business is conducted.

A Jural Assembly is not a Grand Jury. Jural means relating to the rights of law; using the law — recognizing and using the Constitution — recognizing God's Word as law and that our Rights come from God and His Word.

The Jural Assembly is the people who have made their **Declaration of Soverign Rights** and have taken the **Jural Covenant affirmation or oath,** and had them witnessed by two others who are already in, or committing to come into, the Jural Assembly via the two basic documents.

Where there are three interested women or men who want to come into the Republic, they can be the principal and two witnesses for each other. They can establish themselves as qualified women and men to give each other the Jural Covenant oath.

Either way, these new people will need guidance, education, structure, and a plan to follow for growing the Republic in their part of the free state.

In time, much of this can be posted on the Restored Republic website for Educational and Training resources.

## 9
# Begin With The General Assembly

One General Assembly is needed at the state level and additional Jural Assemblies are needed at the county level.

Jural Assemblies are made up of groups of We-The-People who have chosen to be active participants in de jure Grand Juries now being formed all across the land in each of the 50 free states, which comprise **The re-inhabited Republic for the united States of America,** to make it a "beacon light" for the world shining from the heights of God's loving and forgiving grace.

**We-The-People** create the government under which the people in the Republic wish to live.

The **State Jural Assembly** is established by forming a board of directors for **[your] State Jural Assembly** . . .

1. **Ambassador**
2. **Governor**
3. **Attorney General**
4. **Secretary of State**
5. **Recording Secretary**
6. **Treasurer**
7. **Sergeant-at-arms**

The **Ambassador** is the Maine free State's guide.

The **Ambassador** is the original teacher, and **the first County Development Director** for the counties in [your] free State in which he lives.

The **Ambassador** calls together this first **Jural Assembly** in his state.

The **Ambassador** is the connecting link between the Republic at the national level and his independent free state.

The **Regional Ambassador** at the national level of the Republic is responsible for educating and guiding the state Ambassadors in the policies of the Republic in which the 50 free states exist.

The **Governor** autographs, seals, and files the Declarations of Sovereign Rights, and accepts the Jural Covenants for his files.

The **Sergeant-at-Arms** is responsible for the orderly conduct of the meetings and should be familiar with the parliamentary procedures in Robert's Rules of Order, or its equivalent, that you will use in conducting orderly meetings.

**JURAL ASSEMBLIES:**

A **Jural Assembly** is required in each county or group of counties in the free state.

When fully formed, Jural Assemblies must have at least 27 Jurists; 19 seated and 8 alternates. In the meantime, it is lawful for us to work with who we have.

The original Jurists will fill **7 offices** by their choice.
 1. **Jury Foreman**
 2. **Jury Foreman alternate**
 3. **Recording Secretary**
 4. **Corresponding Secretary**
 5. **Treasurer**
 6. **Commissioner**
 7. **Archivist**

The **Commissioner** is charged with seeing that the minimun of 27 Jurists is maintained on his respective Jury.

*All officials are provisional until officially elected.*

**Jural Assemblies** consist of 4 levels of government.

**Level 1: We-The-People** in General Assembly

**Level 2: The Legislature**
- (1) Senator (state)
- (1) Senator (national) (meaning federal)
- (10) Representatives (of We-The-People)

**Level 3: The Executive**
- (1) Governor
- (1) Ambassador
- (1) Attorney General
- (1) Secretary of State

**Level 4: The Judiciary** (2 independent Arms)
**National Judiciary**
- (1) Chief Justice
- (1) Clerk of Court
- (1) Recording Secretary
- (1) Bailiff

**State Judiciary** (the same)
- (1) Chief Justice
- (1) Clerk of Court
- (1) Recording Secretary
- (1) Bailiff

**GRAND JURIES:**

A **Grand Jury** is required in each county or group of counties in the free state.

**Forming The Grand Juries:**

A fully seated Grand Jury consists of 19 seated Jurists and 8 substitutes for the National and State Jural Courts, and each County Court of your free State.

Each Grand Jury requires . . .
1. **Jury Foreman**
2. **Jury Foreman alternate**
3. **Recording Secretary**
4. **Corresponding Secretary**
5. **Treasurer**
6. **Commissioner**
7. **Archivist**

*Everything must be documented for official recognition.*

**The Governor, the two Chief Justices, and the two Jury Foremen cannot maintain two hat;** all others are free to hold multiple offices at first, to be relinquished when others come on board to take their place.

Each General Assembly will eventually require . . .
1. **Chairman**
2. **Chairman alternate**
3. **Recording Secretary**
4. **Corresponding Secretary**
5. **Treasurer**
6. **Archivist**
7. **Sergeant-at-Arms**
8. **Media & PR Director**
9. **Facility Manager**
10. **Education and Training Director**
11. **Judicial Training Director**
12. **Webmaster**

# 10
# Duties & Calls To Action

We-The-People are the AUTHORITY in a Republican Form of Government.

The **General Assembly** "hires and fires" We-The-People's "elected servants" according to the **Policies, Procedures, and Protocol of the General Assembly.**

The **General Assembly** "hires and fires" the state Government officers. The **General Assembly** is the "employer." The "elected officials" are the employees.

This is why the Governor cannot be the one who calls the Assembly together because an employee cannot direct his employer — the **General Assembly** — and tell him what to do.

The Governor cannot be the principle "nation-to-free-state" communication link because he is not in charge of the "We-The-People's" **General Assembly**. The Governor is an employee "hired and fired" by the assembly; as are all other elected, appointed or hired state, county, city, and other local and state level government men and women in the free state.

The **General Assembly** needs an **Ambassador** to call **the first Jural Assembly** together so they can get the initial State Cabinet of officers seated and in place as **a seven-man Administration Board** comprised of a **Governor, Attorney General, Secretary of State, Recording Secretary, Treasurer, Sergeant-at-Arms** (who knows Robert's Rules of Order or the chosen system of order if different),

*Building Blocks of the Republic* 37

and an **Ambassador** to permanently guide them from here on out. (See Chapter 9.)

The **Ambassador** would pull the people back into an organization if they fall apart. The **Ambassador** is to help and guide them in developing the necessary Republican structure of **required documents** when they don't have direction and know what to do, whether it's building the state or county level Jural Assemblies (and later-on city, town, or other levels within the counties of the free state).

Someone has to be the **original "teacher."**

If there were no one to fill this position, We-The-People would not know or have the authority to get ourselves going as the first level of government and as the power-holders of the government branches — or to even tell We-The-People that we hold those positions.

There always needs to be **someone who will take charge** and move the plan and people forward. Someone setting a date time, and place. It's called **planning, organizing** and **action.**

It's up to the **Ambassador** to make sure that all the We-The-People organizations in the Republican Form of Government get formed and sealed and fully informed.

Without **an independent Ambassador** around to present the Republic Plan, continued education and growth of Assemblies, and de jure Grand Juries in all the free state's counties, We-The-People would have no **Leader — as the main Development Director** for the Republican Form of Government within their free states.

**The Ambassador is to . . .**

1. . . . **assist** in originating Assemblies throughout the free state Republics.

2. . . . **call** the State General Assembly (SGA) together for meetings.

3. . . . **administer** the Declaration of Sovereign Rights (DSR) to all interested in joining the republic free state.

4. . . . **grow** county, district, parish, and city Assemblies — and train members of local Assemblies to do the same.

5. . . . **design**, market, setup, and conduct Education and Awareness Seminars in the free state republic.

6. . . . **recruit** and train a team to assist with various projects, activities, and duties; including communication, data quality, and marketing.

7. . . . **participate** in ambassador training events, conference calls, and other meetings.

The Governor cannot call the General Assembly together. That's one of the duties of the Ambassador. The Ambassador is to chair the 1st or 2nd State General Assembly meetings to appoint a State Administration Board who will continue the meetings for We-The-People from then on. The Ambassador is the engine of the train.

The State Ambassador's duty is to build the Republic and complete the task of re-inhabiting the Republic.

The State Legislators are the representative voice of the people.

All former State Ambassadors who wish to hold a national position in another capacity will be given preference for upcoming higher level positions at the national level.

The **Governor** is elected by the State General Assembly which is his employer.

*Building Blocks of the Republic*

The **Governor** cannot be in charge of We-The-People, his employer.

The **Governor** cannot Chair the General Assembly

The people choose who they want to represent themselves; who will be the **Ambassador** who will build the Assemblies in each county by choosing and guiding a **County Development Director,** get the Grand Juries in place, get the Courts in place, teach the people how they are to govern themselves in conjunction with the state-level Assembly and educational resources.

The **Governor** signs and seals the citizens' Declarations of Sovereignty.

The two **State Senators** on the National Congress are appointed by the state legislature per State Constitution.

In the future the two **State Senators** will be "hired and fired" by the state legislature.

The **State Senators** [not the Governor] represent the people of the free state in the Republic and take information back to their state Assembly of which the Governor is a part.

The **Ambassador** represents We-The-People to the Republic.

The word **Republic** refers to the National Governor or Constitution.

The **Chief Justice** for the *Federal court system* in a state is different from the Chief Justice for the *State court system* which begins with a County Court.

**Everyone** living within or near the free state has the right to peacefully assemble and fill out a **Declaration of Sovereign Rights held by Indigenous Power**.

**Everyone** has the right to swear to or affirm the **Jural Covenant** and become a part of the **Free Jural society.**

**Everyone** has the right to send his paperwork to the Governor who is elected by the State General Assembly and have it sealed with his Seal.

We are a **Republic;** not a **Democracy**.

A **Democracy** operates by a majority vote and forces the minority to conform.

A **Republic** operates by a Constitutional Charter which is the Supreme Law of the land.

A **Republic** operates by the "rule of law" by constitutional power delegated to it by sovereign people. Issues are solved by "due process of law" and **tried by juries**, where a jury is the people who delegated constitutional power to the elected officials and who can also withhold power from being exercised on a case by case basis.

A **Republic** operates by **constitutional proceedings** to protect the rights of the minority as well as the rights of the majority.

**Due process of law** must be exercised in removing any Officer or Governor who refuses to serve the people within the geographical boundaries of the state.

**The People** in all the free states are governed by two Constitutions — the Constitution for the state in which they live and the Constitution for the Republic in which the state exists.

**The Republic is not over the State, nor is the State over the Republic** — the Republic and the State work co-equally side-by-side.

Power lies in the People through their Senators and Representatives who they elect to represent them in the Republic and in the republic free states.

**Sheriffs** are the Enforcement Arm of the people, who enforce **the Constitution for the free State** for the people.

*Building Blocks of the Republic*

**Rangers** are the Enforcement Arm of the people, who enforce **the Constitution for the de jure Republic** for the state.

The **Governor** cannot give authority to, nor withhold authority for or from the Rangers in his state because the sovereign people delegate authority to the Rangers via the Constitution for the Republic.

**The Republic is not a sovereign entity; We-The-People are the Sovereigns.**

The framework of our free and independent states, and of the **Republic for the united States of America** has existed here since before any of us were born, and we can **re-inhabit** that which is and was already here.

The **Ambassador program** was established to assist the people in being educated about their rights to assemble and enter the lawful jurisdiction of the Republic and become party to its Constitution.

The **Ambassadors** are qualified to assist people in populating their state for their Republic.

We need **Ambassador's Assistants** in each free state. We should have 10-20 **Ambassador's Assistants** for each large populated area, and a **County Development Director in each county** in order to welcome the flood of people who will be coming into the Republic as events begin to unfold.

## 11
# Forming Jural Assemblies
*( in review )*

**Jural Assemblies** are being established for each State in each county in the State.

Both state-level and county-level Assemblies need Administration.

Jural Assemblies are being administered by the following office holders of each administration board:

1. **Chairman** (someone to chair the Jural Assembly meetings);

2. **Alternate Chairman** (someone to act when the Chairman is absent);

3. **Recording Secretary** (someone to record and keep the minutes of the Jural Assembly meetings.)

4. **Corresponding Secretary** (someone to take care of all emails to the free state's website, to answer, coordinate, and distribute information to necessary people.)

5. **Treasurer** (someone to be the steward of fiscal disbursements and receipts.)

6. **Sergeant-at-Arms** (someone who know *Robert's Rules of Order* and oversees assembly meetings.)

7. **Archivist** (someone who keeps track of all the "joining" documents; oaths; etc. and keeps documents in the National Data Base current; and updates the Jural Assembly Roster with the names and contact information of new members of the Jural Assembly.

8. **Media and PR Director** (someone in charge of the free state's advertising materials; radio, TV; who works with

the webmaster to develop the website information; schedules "seminar presentations" and schedules speakers to go out and give presentations regaring the Reinhabited Republic for the united States of America.)

9. **Facility Manager** (someone who locates and schedules the physical locations for holding Jural Assembly meetings.)

10. **Educational Training Director**

11. **Judicial Training Director**

12. **Webmaster** (someone who manager the website for the republic free state.)

**The Ambassador needs to have an agenda.**

At the Assembly level, the Ambassador needs to call the meeting together at least the first time. **The Ambassador is where the "buck" starts and stops.**

Many positions need to be filled to create and build the Free State Republic. Some people need to wear more than one "hat" until enough other volunteers come on board.

The Ambassador needs to find a first location, set a date and time for the first meeting, and inform all the General and Jural Assemblymen and women of it.

The Ambassador should not be shy about asking others to help him, i.e. delegate tasks to others as required.

After a month, or so, it's up to the newcomer to know the schedules, have a contact with someone else, and become responsible to keep up with what's going on regarding the General and Jural Assembly operations.

The above applies to the Ambassador for the state level assembly, or to the Ambassador helping the Country Development Director get started with the Jural Assemblies in the counties.

## 12
# Forming de jure Grand Juries

There are three categories of Grand Juries in free states.

1. The **National Grand Jury** with its Chief Justice
2. The **State Grand Jury** with its Chief Justice
3. **County Grand Juries** with their Justices

From each state-level or county-level Jural Assembly, recruit men and women of at least 25 years of age to form the de jure Grand Juries, and then those recruits will choose the following seven officers.

1. **Jury Foreman**
2. **Jury Foreman alternate**
3. **Recording Secretary**
4. **Corresponding Secretary**
5. **Treasurer**
6. **Commissioner**
7. **Archivist**

The **Commissioner** is appointed first so he can put the required jurists together. He is on the Grand Jury to keep it together. It is not his responsibility to recruit new jurists. That responsibility falls upon the Ambassador directly and with the associated We-The-People of the Jural Assembly.

Each Commissioner is responsible for only the Grand Jury he is a part of.

The **Ambassador** is the guide who first calls the State Jural Assembly together where everything begins in the free state.

The **Ambassador** appoints **County Development Directors** when enough men and women are available for establishing a Jural Assembly in each County or group of Counties in the free state.

It will then be the responsibility of one of the above mentioned three (Commissioner, Ambassador, County Development Dirctors) to coordinate, organize, and get names on paper for the record. This is why it's a good idea to use a **Roster of Members Names & Contact Information** as one of the joining documents in order to get the names and contact information of the members of the General Assembly and of those willing members to serve on a Grand Jury if and when needed to do so.

The starting positions of the Grand Juries are the two Chief Justices for the two courts, then filling the first Grand Jurist slots for the Federal Grand Jury. Chief justice positions are positions of maturity to be filled with someone who is teachable and has the gift to teach.

Forming the de jure Grand Juries does not fall under the authority of the Governor of the state, nor does the Governor nor anyone else have any authority over de jure Grand Juries. **The Grand Juries are "stand-alone" bodies of volunteers from We-The-People's Jural Assemblies,** who work in conjunction with the Chief Justice of the state and federal jurisdictional Courts.

The Grand Juries come from the We-The-People Jural Assemblies.

The State Ambassador is the main organizer of the people, not only for the state level, but for all of the counties throughout the state as well.

## 13
# Record Keeping By Whom

Let us understand what keeping power and control in the hands of We-The-People is all about.

Recently a long list of documents was sent out to all the free state Governors asking them to supply those documents for the database of the Union of the 50 free states.

The Governor was asked this time to be responsible for this request.

But no one elected into the government of the free state should be the Archivist (record keeper) of the free state, particularly for the foundational documents of We-The-People's Jural Assemblies for the establishment of the people and the documents that create the free state's Republican Form of self-government.

Why?

Because Jural Assembly employees should not have this responsibility. Why would the **parents** (**Jural Assemblies,** the first level of the government in the free state) let their children (**elected government employees**) hold the parents' Marriage Certificate, Birth Certificates, and other valuable papers that document and record the events, policies and positions of their life?

The State's Government Employees, in a free state that has the American Republican Form of self-government, must report directly to Jural Assembly Members. They are to give "progress reports" to the Jural Assembly each time there is a meeting.

*Building Blocks of the Republic*

A precedent needs to be set with their policies — while they are provisional — to know that they need to directly answer on a periodic basis to the faces of the people in the Jural Assemblies, who can fire them for misconduct at any time.

**State Settlement Constitutions** are to be written so that there are "discharge" provisions for misconduct at any time during a term in office, not just in two, four, or six year increments while you the employer suffer; because We-The-People are not in charge. The Jural Assembly holds the reins of the first level of government, by the People, for the People, on the land.

No elected servant has the authority to make "appointments". Every "appointment" must be made and approved by the Jural Assembly. Every servant having authority in state government is directly responsible to the General Assembly, not to a fellow "servant". We must do everything we can to imbed, plant, cement, root and ground **power** and **authority** with **responsibility** and **accountability,** under covenant, in We-The-People's hands.

## 14
# Bureau Of Republic Records

The Bureau of Republic Records is tasked with one function, that is **to unify the "official records" from 50 free states** of the Republic for the united States of America. We do not hold any authority in the creation of, or provide any legal representation of any of the material presented on this web site. That authority is strictly held by "We the People" under the de jure government constitutions by which they are supported and protected.

**All legal advisory and lawful reference is vested in the Judicial System** of the Republic for the united States of America, the One Supreme Court and it's 50 Free State Inferior Courts along with their individual Jural Societies.

The Bureau of Republic Records has been established in an effort to maintain the integrity and unification of the re-inhabited Republic's individual records. Here American Nationals of the Republic have the ability to retrieve up-to-date official records and documents.

The Bureau of Republic Records was also created to formulate and establish a census report for the documentation of all the American Nationals of the Republic. As the number of documented American Nationals grows, our International and National voices resounding as "One" will declare and ensure our Sovereign Rights as appointed by our heavenly Father, and we will be recognized internationally for **uninhibited lawful travel** across all borders.

By bearing in mind that *"Every kingdom divided against itself is brought to desolation: and every city or house divided against itself shall not stand"* (Matthew 12:25), we are reminded that **we should continually seek unification and not division,** most certainly under the guidance of our Lord.

## 15
# Duties Of The Commissioner

It is the **Commissioner's** responsibility to appoint a **Director of Judicial training** to do training, and to keep 27 on the Grand Jury — 19 seated voting jurists and 8 alternates, appointed from those in the Jural Assembly who are eligible and willing to serve.

Free states need to have a **Director of Judicial training** — one to go to training seminars, such the one given recently in Atlanta, and come back to his free state, to disseminate what he has learned for all the Grand Jurists of the Grand Juries and the Courts.

The **Commissioner** will keep a roster of who is and who is not trained in order for those jurists to be qualified to sit on a Grand Jury.

The **Commissioner** will help the state-level **Judicial Training Director** and his team set up county and regional training classes, and be responsible for having qualified Grand Jury jurists on the Grand Jury at all times.

The general population of the **We-The-People Jural Assembly jurists** should have this learning available to them. This is all part of the larger picture of educating all the people of America.

The de jure Grand Jury is **bottom-up government** in the **American Republican system of government** by the people, **the creators of our government,** in absolute control.

## 16
## Law of the Land Or Law of the Sea

**Common Law** is the law of the land which refers to the living, breathing, human being, while **Statutory Law** is the law of the sea (maritime law) which is the law of contracts which applies to commerce and corporations.

The purveyors of **Statutory Law** — parliaments and governments — invented **"fake persons"** (corporations) to which their **"fake laws"** could apply. This is the **Strawman** (a legal fiction) which is created, in your name, in all capital letters.

**John Doe** and derivatives like **John L. Doe, or John Leslie of the Doe family,** are — under Common Law — the living, breathing, human being with a soul.

**JOHN DOE** is the **"legal person/fiction/corporation/trust"** created under the jurisdiction of **Statutory Contract Law**.

When government agencies — law enforcement, legal and financial, etc. — communicate with you they always print your name in all capital letters because they are not writing to you, *the living being,* but to the artificial **Strawman, the corporation of one,** that was created in your name when you were born.

Their trick is to keep you believing — throughout your whole life — that **John Doe** and **JOHN DOE** mean the same thing. **Well they don't!**

It is very important to understand that all **governments** — your local council, courts, police force, and so on — **are private corporations**.

*Building Blocks of the Republic*

If you should check this out with **Dun and Bradstreet,** which provides credit information on businesses and corporations worldwide, this would be confirmed.

The UNITED STATES CORPORATION and the UNITED KINGDOM CORPORATION are both in Chapter 11 Bankruptcy.

This is a state of bankruptcy which "**...allows businesses to reorganize themselves, giving them an opportunity to restructure debt and get out from under certain burdensome leases and contracts.**

"**Typically a business is allowed to continue to operate while it is in Chapter 11 bankruptcy, although it does so under the supervision of the Bankruptcy Court and its appointees.**"

So who controls the "**Bankruptcy Court and its appointees**" which is currently "**supervising**" the "**government corporations**" called the **UNITED STATES INC.** and the **UNITED KINGDOM INC**?

**The House of Rothschild** — *and its International Banking Cartel.*

## 17
# Historical Note

The organization of de jure Grand Juries began in February, 2010, when Mr. James Timothy Turner appointed a **State Cordinator** to establish the first 27-member de jure Grand Jury in America. By the end of the following month, de jure Grand Juries were established in all 50 states of the Union.

Of the first 27 members chosen, 19 are still "seated voting members" with 6 of them elected as Grand Jury officers. The other 8 are still alternates.

During the following months, from March to July, people coming into the free state Republic became part of a growing "jury pool" for the Grand Jury that was the power of the organization. This Grand Jury was and is the engine of the train.

A **Jury Foreman** and a **Foreman pro tem** (alternate) conducted the meetings.

Our Nebraska group meetings were held with a formal agenda, one night a week, every other week, from 6:30 to 11:00 oclock, p.m.

The **Grand Jury Recorder** took the minutes, the **Corresponding Secretary** followed up with new people in our state who signed up on a nation-wide website.

The **Treasurer** kept track of donations, and a **Commissioner** was in charge of having 19 on a roster of seated, voting **de jure Grand Jury members**, plus 8 **alternates** — and training. Most of the information was provided at that time by the national level via nation-wide conference calls lasting from 1 to 4 hours long.

*Building Blocks of the Republic*

The Jury Foreman Counted as one of the original 27 Jurists. The State Coordinator was to be one of the alternates which were gradually listed as inactive alternates when others could fill the 27 Grand Jury slots. In some other cases, there were personality, authority or power conflicts between State Coordinators and the Foreman. Not everyone stepped into this with a servant's heart!

Then in July/August we were told that we needed to sever from the **Restore America Plan** (RAP). There's a longer story in this which we won't explain here.

As a result, **the State Coordinator's title was changed to Ambassador,** and the formation of the body of We-The-People who were participating in the **Republican Form of Government** was now called an **"Assembly"** of which the Grand Jury would become the **Judicial Arm** of the Free State Government WITHIN the Assembly. This meant that **The "We-The-People Jural Assembly"** was now the engine driving the train, and the elected officials for the state governments travelled in each of the cars.

At the time when the State Coordinators became Ambassadors, many State Coordinators became Governors. The properly seated ones were "elected," but some appointed themselves into that position if there was a weak "Assembly" in that free state. These particular ones hadn't been having Assembly meetings so they lost interest and fell apart.

Around October, 2010, several Governors felt as if the Ambassador position was a "federal agent" within "their state", because to get things going, in the beginning, the **State Coordinator** was appointed by Tim Turner. The **State Coordinator** was called a **Guardian Elder** at that time (there were four men), and the jurisdiction of **"National"** wasn't yet in our program. Then in July through August, when the elections for Mr. James Tim Turner as provisional President, and Mr. Charles Eugene Wright as provisional Vice President, plus five Supreme Court Justices, and the President's Cabinet was established, now **"National jurisdiction"** entered the picture.

If there's a change today as to whom the Ambassador of a free state is, coordination and approval is in the hands of the **Chief Ambassador for the Republic**.

This is not a "National level" position, he is simply **the main coordinator** "in charge" of the 50 state Ambassadors. You can't have structure and organization without "SOMEONE being in charge; someone to take responsibility for the "buck stops here" decisions.

But the greatest need is simply for someone who other Ambassadors can go to for advice, suggestions, counsel, etc. All fifty Ambassadors cannot reach the President directly, but **the main coordinator** can. That's the Biblical idea and principle of leadership.

At no time did any State Coordinator (now **Ambassador**) ever believe he was a "federal-level" representative within a state!

The only "national" connection is simply that the **State Ambassador** is the "main communication link" between national **Interim President Tim Turner** and any other national messenger representing We-The-People.

President Turner does not want the **Governor** to be the recipient of national communications in place of the **Ambassador** because this by-passes the **We-The-People Jural Assembly** which is the creator of government and therefore the **main governing authority in the state**.

*Building Blocks of the Republic* 57

Re-inhabiting the Republic re-establishes We-The-People as the First Level of Government. This means "keeping the power in the hands of the people", as not only a belief in the "head," but as something to be lived out in one's actions.

The documents should help everyone understand how that this is done.

# 18
# Sample Constituion

**WE-THE-PEOPLE** of the Maine Republic, in Jural Assembly lawfully convened on the land of the de jure republic of original jurisdiction, in concert with the lawfully assembled national Republic for the united States of America, have hereby and of the date entered herein below, established this constitution as the foundational basis of the reassembled Maine Republic, for the intent and purposes as further described below.

For exigent purposes and to provide for the immediate establishment by constitution of the lawful assembly of the Sovereign People of this republic, this constitution has been established on the Eighth Day of the Second Month in the Year of our Lord Two Thousand Eleven. This constitution shall serve as an interim foundational document until such time as it is replaced by a more complete version as provided for herein below.

### Article One: Legislative Powers
**Section 1**: The legislative powers delegated by this Constitution shall be vested in a General Assembly of the Maine Commonwealth Republic and shall consist of Statesmen and a House of Delegates. Each county shall send one statesman and two delegates to the General Assembly.

### Article Two: Executive Powers
**Section 1**: The supreme executive powers delegated by this Constitution shall be vested in a Governor of the Maine Commonwealth Republic.

### Article Three: Judicial Powers

**Section 1**: The judicial powers delegated by this Constitution shall be vested in a Chief Supreme Court Justice in the Maine Commonwealth Republic. Additional Supreme Court Justices shall be provided for below.

### Article Four: County Sheriffs

**Section 1**: As provided for in the County Settlement Constitutions, County Sheriffs shall be chosen by the people of each county.

### Article Five: Militia

**Section 1**: Mainers shall maintain the right to be armed and disciplined for their own defense, called to action by order of the County Sheriff. Those who conscientiously scruple not to bear arms shall not be compelled to do so. The militia officers shall be appointed in such manner, and for such time, as shall be directed by law.

### Article Six: County Assemblies and County Offices

**Section 1**: The building blocks of the Maine Republic shall be the County Assemblies established by the Sovereign People of the counties of Maine. By reference, the County Settlement Constitutions are recognized and included herewith in this Maine Commonwealth Republic constitution.

**Section 2**: Each county shall elect office holders to fill the offices as provided for in the county constitutions. After all counties have elected and filled such offices, the Chief Justices of the County Supreme Courts shall convene to elect the members of the Republic Supreme Court. Other republic level bodies and offices may also be filled from the ranks of county level elected office holders.

### Article Seven: Confirmation of Unalienable Rights

**Section 1:** The enumeration of unalienable rights contained within the County Settlement Constitution template is included herein and thereby confirmed for the Maine Republic by reference and confirmation.

### Article Eight: Committee for Preparing a Permanent Constitution

The People of this republic assembled due to the current national and global conditions that prevail at this time have entered this current constitution under exigent circumstances that of necessity have forced immediate establishment hereof. Therefore, upon ratification of this constitution, a committee shall be selected and empowered to prepare a more expanded constitution within the proceeding ninety (90) days, or less, and upon completion, to be presented to the lawfully convened Jural Assembly of the Maine Republic, for review, discussion, vote and ratification. If upon ratification by the People this current document shall be superseded by the newly ratified constitution.

### Article Nine: Temporary Adoption of Original 1849 Constitution

The Constitution of the united States of America, at Article 4 Section IV states: The United States shall guarantee to every State in this Union a Republican Form of Government, and shall protect each of them against invasion; and upon Application of the Legislature, or of the Executive (when the Legislature cannot be convened) against domestic violence.

So that no inconvenience may arise from the alterations and amendments while transitioning from the interim MAINE STATE Constitution to a Republican Form of Government by and through this Constitution of the Maine Republic, and any subsequent constitutions lawfully entered by the People, and in order to carry out the same into complete operation as determined from time to time by the legislative powers of the Maine Constitution, it is hereby declared and ordained:

We hereby adopt and ratify the original 1820 Maine Constitution as our interim provisional Constitution to be attached and made a part hereof, until such time as the above established committee is able to review said original constitution, other state/republic constitutions and whatever other sources for the preparation of the permanent constitution to be submitted by the Jural Assembly of the People of the Maine commonwealth Republic.

**We-The-People of the Maine Commonwealth Republic,** having convened in Jural Assembly on this Eleventh Day of February in the Year Two Thousand Eleven, and having reviewed this instrument and found it to be proper and acceptable for the purposes as stated herein, have by majority vote ratified this Constitution for the Maine Republic.

_____

governor's autograph, date, and seal

## 19
# Sample Declaration Of Intention

**WE THE PEOPLE of the Maine republic** in conjunction with the constitution of this republic as put forth, ratified and accepted by the People in Lawful Assembly, do hereby attach thereto this **Declaration of Intention** as an addendum thereof, to establish the intention of this Assembly to be known to other republics of this National Republic and to the People of the world.

It is our heartfelt and fully considered opinion that it is not enough to simply provide for the benefit and well-being of ourselves, our families and our local assemblies, but to see to the greater good in creating an environment of abundance, prosperity and well-being for all individuals in our society, in our nation, and throughout our world. Based on such, we are moved by our conscience and the spirit that moves through us to hereby proclaim our intentions, to wit:

We recognize the unalienable sanctity of life of all men, women and children, and further recognize that such sanctity of life is debased and compromised without the safeguards and protections that we by right have established by the constitution of our republic and those of the other republics with which we have joined in national union. Yet there are many in this republic and across the nation, and many more still throughout our world as a whole, who have been so debased and compromised; therefore, we declare our intention by the following words to work in concert together in our local assemblies, our republic and with all those of like-mind and spirit as is expressed in the following words.

It is the intention of this Maine Republic to be so constituted, and to thereby, as an assembly of Free Men and Women, founded upon the Law of the Land, establish for ourselves, our families, our communities, and our republic a balanced system of self-governance, in divine converse with the unified and collective spirit that guides each of us in our personal and sacred relationship with our Creator, and to be a vehicle for the indwelling presence of the living and eternal being thereof, and dedicate our republic upon two principles as foundational matters of purpose and intent.

**The first such principle** is that of **Service** to the yet larger whole of the human race currently endowed with the divinely bestowed Gift of Life here upon Planet Earth. Such intent of service is founded upon the primary recognition that each individual who walks upon this Earth is a sacrament between the individual and his or her Creator, generally understood by all as a prime source and the fount of all blessings of life. We firmly hold that such a gift of life thusly bestowed shall be always and forever safeguarded as such a sacrament, to be honored in all thoughts, acts, deeds and intentions by all others who share the common ground of life on this Earth, embodied and endowed with the sacred breath that we all share. We find within our hearts to declare that we intend to be in service to protect and preserve such sanctity of life as the highest calling that any one individual or the aggregate whole of our society assembled in republic can pursue and defend and thus we so declare that this is our intention.

**The second such principle** that we declare and recognize as the guiding foundation upon which our republic shall be constituted is that of **Stewardship**, herein defined as the balanced and integrated approach towards the development and maintenance of the necessities of Life in all of its manifold expression through the natural resources with which our Divine Creator has so endowed this Earth for our sustenance, support, nurturing and well-being. As such, our focus shall be as a fiduciary responsibility in relationship to the natural resources that come under our purview, to hold, maintain, develop and expand said resources for the benefit of all who are in this republic, for all who walk side-by-side with us in this journey of life, and for all of humankind in general. We hereby declare that we shall be guided in our endeavors with a sense of sacredness for the Gifts of Life, that all current and future generations shall be the beneficiaries of our service in stewardship of all the resources that have been designed by Our Creator to provide all of the requirements of life for a whole, balanced and joyfully blessed journey on this planet. In essence, we declare herein the recognition that all such Divine Gifts require an integrated co-creative relationship between Our Source and Ourselves as the stewards of this Earth.

Therefore, we put forth and declare this intention of **Service** and **Stewardship** to be the foundation upon which our republic shall be built. As such we recognize that all men, women and children are endowed with their own sovereign power and authority within a co-equal relationship between the Earth as our home, our Creator as our Source, and ourselves as divine spirits in corporeal form. We also declare our recognition of the Earth as the living biosphere that sustains our lives and those lives of all the plant and animal kingdoms that share this planet with humankind as a part of the larger blessing of wholeness we each have been endowed with by the eternal and infinite Source of Life that has placed us here to imbibe and embrace the gifts of life we share. In sacred communion with Source, Spirit, and this Earth, we declare that our efforts shall go forth tirelessly to bring into manifestation fulfillment in our world based on equality, abundance, compassion, mercy and reverence for the sacredness of all Life that shall emerge forthwith by our efforts and our intentions. With Heaven and Earth as our eternal witnesses this day we proclaim that we shall not stop until all of this is fulfilled in our lifetime so that all may share the peace and abundance that is assuredly the birthright of all humankind. We place at the highest level our reverence for the sanctity of all beings, the integrity of all life, and the sovereignty and indivisible wholeness of indwelling spirit through which we honor ourselves, each other, and all other life forms of this Earth.

We declare our intention to support, nurture and defend the rights of all human beings who walk upon this Earth with whom we share the Gift and Breath of Life. This intention is founded upon the recognition that all human beings are endowed with the unalienable rights of self-determination and the fundamental assurances of the minimum qualities of life. We firmly hold that such assurances of the minimum qualities of life can only be fulfilled by having the necessities such as proper nourishment, clothing, shelter, access to knowledge and education, training for fulfilling capacities to support and sustain their lives and their families, and to be integrated within their relationships of social, spiritual, economic, familial and community bonds. We further recognize the sanctity of all sentient beings that share an alignment with this declaration and with divine integrity in these principles. It is our dedicated intention that we shall strive to assist all those in need in order that they may provide for themselves and their families the means of establishing the fundamental requirements of life while on this Earth. We shall be guided by our consciences to honor all life forms and all human beings on our planet, and all sentient beings in the universe at large that support and align with these principles and intentions. We are guided by such principles and we shall strive continuously to apply our efforts to uplift and sustain the qualities of life that we wish to have for ourselves, our families, our communities, our republic, our nation and our world, and to continue in our efforts until all on this planet have achieved such a goal.

We come forward in Peace, with no other agenda except for those herein declared, and thereby maintaining the respect and honoring of all human beings, male and female in full equality, of all races, religions, political organizations, and any other human aggregations that we would desire and expect for ourselves. In this regard we declare our intention to honor all sentient beings with whom we might interact and to hold at the highest level of respect the free moral agency with which every being has been endowed by their Creator and True Source. By this declaration of intention we ask of each individual who wishes to enter into this society and republic that they examine their own conscience and personal commitment to this **Declaration of Intention**, and in the innermost chamber of their hearts consider joining this pledge to uphold and fulfill this solemn covenant to the best of their capabilities. We hereby invite all those individuals on this planet who also wish to undertake such a pledge to join with us on an equal footing, in sovereign and unalienable capacity, as we are intended to be by our Creator, our Primary Source and the only authority to whom we must answer.

In sacred communion, we hereby declare that we shall

be guided by the inspirational words to be found in a little known document which formalized the union of the Polish and Lithuanian states in Central Europe in the year of 1413, known as the **Act of Union**, wherein it is stated:

*"It is known to all that a Man [or Woman] will not attain salvation if he [or she] is not sustained by Divine Love, which does no wrong, radiates goodness, reconciles those in discord, unites those who quarrel, dissipates hatred, puts an end to anger, furnishes for all the food of Peace."*

*"Through that Love, laws are established, kingdoms are maintained, cities are set in order, and the well-being of the State is brought to the highest level. May this Love make us equal, whom Spirit and Identity of laws and privileges have already joined."*

To this declaration of purpose and intent, we dedicate our creative force and capacities, our considered commitment and resolve, our heartfelt passions and our very breath of life to see such as this fulfilled in our time. We hereby affirm and declare that all Life is intended to be filled with unlimited abundance and prosperity, to be free to enjoy the abundant fruits of creation as designed and manifested through our collective and infinite source. Such abundance shall ensue from the Infinite and Sacred Heart outwards into the manifest world, for it is hereby decreed by this **Declaration of Intention** that there shall never abide any structure of lack, poverty or limitation that would inhibit the free flow of our Source's infinite pleasure in bringing forth a true cornucopia of abundance, prosperity and joy on this Earth.

**We the People of the Maine Republic** shall forever be aligned to this intention, so that the people in lawful assembly in community, republic and nation shall forever fill and overflow, spreading to all whom we touch the divine nectar of Life, Liberty, and Freedom, and in such radiance shall each of us become a center point of infinite joy.

IN WITNESS WHEREOF, in the presence of our Divine Counselor and Guiding Light, the True Source of Eternal Life, the Supreme Being with whom we hereby establish this covenant and co-creative bond, we do hereby set our Hands and Seals and subscribe to this **Declaration of Intention** and to the Pledge and Principles contained herein and offer it forthwith to our conjoined fellow men and women in republic and our One Nation Assembled in Union and to the world in whole.

_____
governor's autograph, date, and seal

*The following chapters are adapted from a speech given by the Chief Justice of the Republic of California Supeme Court, <u>Justice Ken Cousens,</u> at the recent California Freedom Jamboree.*

# 20
# Quick Lesson In Politics

What is the difference between a Republic and a Democracy?

Well, the difference between a Republic and a Democracy is like 3 wolves and a sheep coming together to form a government. In a Democracy the majority rules as to what's for dinner. In a Republic the 3 wolves must absolutely protect the rights of the sheep. The rights and capacity and standing in law of one man or woman in a Republic is stronger than 300 million people in a Democracy.

On the other hand of course, 300 million people in a Republic can transform this world. Even 1 million people in a Republic can literally transform our country and transform this world.

The reasons is, in a Republic we are the law. That doesn't mean anarchy, which is the lack of the law, lack of authority, chaos; it means an orderly coming together in a social compact in which the rights of the individual are paramount. And the capacity of the individual to hold the grounding in law is also supreme.

We Want to be at home in this world. We want to establish this world as our home. We want to be at home everywhere in this world. And to do so, we must figure out what is wrong, because in our home it is not acceptable for people to be starving. It is not acceptable for people in our home to be suffering the way billions of people suffer on this planet.

I grew up believing, as I was told, that this was the greatest county in the world.

As I grew and explored what was going on in this world, what was going on in this country, I came to understand that, at one and the same time, we are the greatest country in the world, but at the same time we are the most rogue state on this planet, that is purposely pursuing an agenda that is not protecting the rights of the sheep, but trying and intending to have that sheep for dinner.

The sheep is the people, obviously, of this world.

So part of my exploration was trying to understand, how could a very small number of people, just a few thousand of people, control 6 billion people. It doesn't make sense, except for one thing that I have seen is, believe it or not, it is our acceptance — our consent!

I do not agree! I don't accept and allow this anymore! That's powerful!

When two stand up, it's even more powerful! But when thousands, and millions of people stand up and come together they cannot be stopped!

Another thing I like to do is put jig-saw puzzles together. The more complex the better I like it. And I didn't realize it at the time, but I was training myself to look at complex multi-layered structures, and how to see the implicate order, the template of the emerging picture.

Because, as you know, a jig-saw puzzle as a picture, and the goal is to put it all together so you can see the whole picture.

But there are layers of encoding in that picture puzzle. There are the shapes, the colors, the design, and as it emerges, you see a correlative template of the whole picture coming together.

So when I set out to find out what was wrong in this world, I started exploring, what were those multilayered levels?

And about 20 years ago, I started studying law. And law became the galvanizing focus of understanding how this world has been put together to be controlled and actually owned by a very small number of people.

As I describe it, history is the story of the evolution of something we call law, and there is an underlying real law, a standard, we call it God's law, Natures law, that's in balance, that honors all being, honors all life. But in the course of history, that foundation of law has been turned upside down and inside out. What we have is the similitude in the mirror image which is the reverse of real law.

So history is the evolution of law that has evolved to the point where it's been usurped and turned inside out and upside down. And out of that system of distorted, or mirror image law, has come something which we call "money".

The history of law and money has been utilized as a very complex codified system to do what? To bind the people of this planet, and use the people to harvest the natural resources and have the labor and intellectual capacity of the people with those resources to literally build and pay for our own prison.

But the ultimate sense is that we retain the capacity, and we live in a country that has established itself on fundamental foundations.

What is the authority? Who give us the right or the authority to come together and do what we are doing?

In the 1770's the Declaration of Independence of the united State of America was unanimously set forth before institute new government, laying its foundation on such principles and organizing its powers in such form, as to them shall seem most likely to effect their safety and happiness. Prudence, indeed, will dictate that governments long established should not be changed for light and transient causes; and accordingly all experience has shown that mankind are more disposed to suffer, while evils are sufferable, than to right themselves by abolishing the forms to which they are accustomed. But when a long train of abuses and usurpations, pursuing invariably the same object evinces a design to reduce them under absolute despotism, it is their right, it is their duty, to throw off such government, and to provide new guards for their future security."

We are not here to destroy anything. We are in fact at peace with THE UNITED STATES.

We are neutral and we are non-belligerent. We are here to live and co-exist, because we have the inherent right, as this document has established and has been accepted by the world, to reconstitute our own form of self-determination and self-governance to abolish that government and establish a new government on a foundation of principles and policies in which we conscientiouly believe.

This document has never been negated, it is the foundation upon which this country has been built.

So the Republic has been established by lawful process as has been stated before and stated over and over again.

# 21
# The Initial Process

How did this process take place?

All 50 of the states existing in this Union established a Jural Body. The word "Jural" comes from the word "jure" or "Juris". It means "law".

A lawful body was established as a de jure Grand Jury in each of the 50 states. It doesn't matter the size. It matters the holding and the grounding in law. You can read through all the documents and founding structures of law in this country and you will come to understand that when something is brought together properly and lawfully, it rises above any of the things that you think could negate or would prevent it from taking place.

Remember, I said that one person in a Republic is more capable in law than 300 million in a Democracy.

So all 50 states formed a jural body with capacity in law as a de jure Grand Jury.

In **American Juris Prudence** there is a set of documents, volumes called **Corpus Juris Secundum**. "Corpus Juris" means the body of law. "Secundum" is the 2nd or the 2nd Edition. In Volume 38, section A, there's a line or a clause that states that *"When a de jure Grand Jury is formed, a de facto Grand Jury cannot coexist with it."* So the de jure Grand Juries that were formed in February through March of last year (2010) established the re-institution of the law form for the People buy the People and for the People.

This took place in February and March and in late March, unanimously, that body — the 50 Grand Juries — made presentments to the de facto Governors of the 50 states. And it was basically not a demand for them to step down, but was a demand that they take an oath in law to the People, because, as you will come to understand, the government system that is in place, that we've grown used to, it is not based on a pledge or oath to the People and the original structure upon which this country was founded.

This was a presentment in law, and according to every level and rule and regulation in our system, in three days (72 hours) if they did not respond and if they didn't comply, they defaulted on that demand.

When they defaulted, that default was, in effect, an abandonment of their standing in law that had been previously accepted by the People and allowed.

By that abandonment, the People, the de jure Grand Juries of the 50 states, were given the capacity and the full right in law *to institute a new form of self-government and self determination.*

That took place over the next few months leading to the point when we once again — as fifty sovereign bodies with lawful Jural authority and intent — came together and as fifty sovereign bodies established the **First step** in re-instituting the **Republic for the United states of America.** That step was to establish the provisional **executive branch** and to elect President James Timothy Turner to that position, and Charles Wright to the position of Vice President. And progressively from that time in July, through August, September, and October, various other steps were taken. Each state elected a governor, as you know, We elected a Congress and members of the Senate, We convened properly the Congress which led up to that event in November in Utah where we established — by Declaration of Sovereign Intent — who and what we are.

This act has gone out to the world and the world is paying attention. That rogue state known as the corporate UNITED STATES has been on a rampage for decades and even centuries. And the world has had enough. You can see it in the news.

Egypt is exploding because they've had enough. Many nation states have all had enough because they recognize that we've been bamboozled. There is enough wealth on this planet so that no one needs to go hungry, no one needs to live in the kind of abject poverty that we see every day on our TV's.

What I've learned in looking at the codified, multilayered, system of control on this planet is that a big lie has been told to We-The-People and we, unknowingly, confirm the lie.

That lie uses multiple threats to define our reality. Those threats are based on survival and fear. And when we buy into that world that we see today, that world will continue the way it is, on the path to self-destruction.

However, the Republic has committed itself to a new set of principles and policies upon which we will form a new type of governance.

For me those principles are **unity, abundance,** and **prosperity** because there is enough energy in this world, enough wealth in this world, enough water in this world, enough food in this world, so that everybody can have a proper level of nourishment, housing, everything that we take for granted that we cherish for ourselves, for our children, our families, and our communities.

## 22
# Ken Cousen's Declaration Of Intent

Earlier this year in our Jural Assembly in California, I presented a document that I had written 10 years ago. It was called a declaration of intent. It was very simple based on two basic principles: **Service and Stewardship,** and what we see running rampant in the world today is that the resources and the wealth of the world — and I'm not talking about communism or statism or socialism — but about a proper balance in stewardship of the wealth and the resources that can be used for everybody's benefit today.

And we unanimously accept and passed that declaration of intent which was simply that as we build and grow this Republic the wealth that we accrue and build is going to grow and overflow, and spread, across this nation and revitalize it and heal it and bring work to the people and give them what they need to have abundant lives and lives that have meaning and purpose and intent and then America can return to the greatness that we once had and the respect that this world had.

So if those principles mean something to you, please come into the Republic and help us out.

You need to first enter the Republic by one simple act — that act is your individual **Declaration of Sovereign Right held by Indigenous Powers.**

What does that mean?

It means that the people of America have always been the Sovereign. There is no body above the Sovereign other than the Creator. There is no one who tells you what to do. It doesn't look like that's the kind of system we have working today, does it?

Our sovereign rights never went away. They can't go away. If you understand law and history the way we've studied it, you'll understand that the system we're talking about has only been an overlay that was like a blanket laid over the original structure. That structure has never gone away. All we needed to do was re-inhabit it. So the **first step** is the individual. **The first step starts with you.** The building block of the Republic is the individual, you.

**I declared my sovereign rights held by indigenous power.**

What is Indigenous Power? Indigenous means native, native to the land. This doesn't mean that the native Americans — the original first nations in America — are separate from what we're doing. History has brought us to where we are today. We are co-equal with the native Americans. We all hold indigenous power. I honor and respect the native Americans, as I honor and respect all nations, all races. We are co-equal, as we all hold our individual **sovereign rights in indigenous power.**

Therefore, some very educated individuals in law have come together in the nation and at the state level to bring a very simple mechanical way by which everyone can come into the Republic. And that way is defined in two very simple documents.

Your **Declaration of Sovereign Rights** held on the land and a **Jural Covenant** which declares that you have become the law and you create and act your convenant with all of us as we hold the law together.

So as we hold the law together and we are grounded in the law, when we have to create document forms in which we establish our model of self-governance, which is what we are in the process of doing. It's a long hard process. And we need everyone who has a sense of what's going on, on the dark side of things, and while we have the enduring capacity and potentiality to create here in the Republic, to come on board, cause it's time, and that's what this Jamboree is all about.

We're here to bring and welcome people in and establish an understanding of what the solutions to our world problems are.

**Where is the Remedy? How do we fix the problems?**

So the first step is we come individually in. We come into the law and we hold our capacity and standing in law — the Jural Covenant — then we come together as a free state.

California is now established as a free state. That was done by the de jure Grand Jury, and the process that has taken place during the last 10 months. There is nothing that can negate that fact or stop that, or make it not a fact.

So now what we're doing in California is we're convening our counties.

The counties are the building blocks of our Republic — our free state Republic.

The convening of the Jural Assembly of Riverside County — the de jure lawful County — and we ratified the Constitution for that County — its called a **County Settlement Constitution.**

It's a very simple document and if you'll look on the Republic website, you will find it, and you can read it. It has been accepted by numerous counties in California and throughout the national Republic of the nation.

So the county becomes the form of local government.

And the county that forms and establishes the **County Settlement** established officers. And we elect our county officers.

This is important because the REMEDY that we use to get free from this tyrannical despotic parasite known as the federal government, in all of its permutations, and believe me, everything you see down to your local boards of supervisors, and the board of education is a part of the federal government.

So when we establish ourselves at the county level we establish our official seat, we fill those offices and we begin to build our REMEDY.

Why is that? Because some of those offices are such things as a Land Records Office — a Library of Records — **because in law everything is by a record.**

A common law court proceeds on this basis as a **permanent court of record.**

Once you have had to deal with the de facto court system, you know that it's all convoluted. It's all distorted, it's all smoke and mirrors. And if you knew history and law for the past 200 years — as I do — you would faint — if you knew how insidious the nature of that is.

And progressively as we build the California Republic Website and the Republic for the United states' Website there's going to be more and more education on those websites, and I encourage you to utilize these websites for additional information.

**Ignorance and self-government cannot co-exist together.**

If you're ignorant, you're going to be controlled. If you want to stand in **self-responsibility**, and **self-governance**, and **self-determination** collectively as we're doing in the Re-the world and declared:

"When, in the course of human events, it becomes necessary for one people to dissolve the political bands which have connected them with another, and to assume among the powers of the earth, the separate and equal station to which the laws of nature and of nature's God entitle them, a decent respect to the opinions of mankind requires that they should declare the causes which impel them to the separation."

This was written 240 years ago, but it is precisely that which is happening today. It is the basis and the foundation of the authority that We The People have, because this is a foundational document that has never been challenged, has never been negated, and it has been sustained by over 200 years of our history here in America and throughout the world. It is probably the most respected document on this planet.

It goes on to say . . .

"We hold these truths to be self-evident, that all men are created equal, that they are endowed by their Creator with certain unalienable rights — (*unalienable means that they cannot be suspended, they cannot be attached, they cannot be utilized for anything other than the inherent intrinsic capacity of the individual to have life, and liberty, and land, and freedom*) — that among these are life, liberty and the pursuit of happiness. That to secure these rights, governments are instituted among men, deriving their just powers from the consent of the governed. That whenever any form of government becomes destructive to these ends, it is the right of the people to alter or to abolish it, and to public, you must become educated, and it is a lifetime pursuit.

We must do our best to educate others to understand what this means for their freedom and while we need to do the establishment of the Library of Record, the Land Records, the offices at the county level are paramount in creating enough sufficiency to have our REMEDY in law.

We are putting together everything we need to gain the complete remedy to stop mortgage fraud, to stop the foreclosures, to stop the rape and pillage through taxation, how to build a new economy.

## 23
# Quick Lesson In The Economy

Let me give you a quick lesson in economics.

I gave you a quick lesson in politics with the wolves and the sheep.

There's a guy who walks into a hotel. He asks the proprietor, "I would like a room, but can I see it first?"

The proprietor says, "here's a key, go up to the third floor and take a look at the room, but I need a $100 deposit."

So the guy pulls out a $100 bill and puts it on the counter, takes the key, and goes upstairs to checkout the room.

Well, the proprietor of the hotel grabs that $100 bill, runs across the street to the butcher, because he owes him $100, and he pays his bill.

The butcher, in turn, runs across the other street to the carpenter, who just built something in the back room, because he owes him $100, so he pays off the carpenter.

The carpenter happened to visit one of the working ladies of the town, because he owed her $100, so he runs over to her place and pays her off.

Well, her place of business was located in the hotel, so she runs over to the hotel and pays off her bill there.

Just then, the guy comes down from upstairs and says that the room is just not right for me and he takes what he thinks is his $100 bill and leaves.

See how a fair and just economy works?

I think it was James Madison who said something to the effect of — something about our ignorance of coin, credit, and currency, *"We've been bamboozelled as to how that works."*

This is an example of how a fair economy through currency circulation works. That same $100 bill settled four debts. Right?

But what if there was an IRS agent at every step of the way, and he took his 10%, and this one took his 10%, and this one took his 10%, and this one took his 10%? — Because this is how it works.

The non-federal Federal Reserve "Bank" issues a $100 Federal Reserve Note (FRN) out of nothing and SELLS it to the Treasury for a $100 Treasury Bill or Bond, that carries interest attached to all the people through the bondage I made reference to before.

And that Federal Reserve Note is a note that has to someday be repaid. It's an obligation to pay it back to the non-federal Federal Reserve for profit "Bank".

But in the system we have today, it can circulate as a medium of legal tender, but to use it is a privilege, it's a compelled benefit, and when you take a compelled benefit or a privilege from the federal government, you are supposedly [by them] bound by its rules. That supposedly attaches you to everything they call law, but is nothing more than private corporate rules. And if the benefit is a compelled benefit, **this is the basis of fraud.**

The difference is that in order for you to use that $100 bill, you are expected to pay a "use" fee, i.e. a tax. And that $100 bill will become gross income to dozens of people and businesses throughout the country in one year's time, each one of which are expected [by them] to pay, say 10% as an average, of income tax.

Before you know it, the Federal Reserve and its partners have conjured [conned] $200 worth of labor and value on that piece of paper through fraudulent taxation, not to mention inflation and everything else, and it never has to accept repayment of the note, because the note circulates as a means to continually bind and bond and parasitically draw off of our capacity.

So imagine, if we go back to an original economic form where the monetary unit that we use in the Republic is like the first example shown where there is no taxation on the labor or the materials or the wealth that we draw from the land, and we start building a NEW economic foundation.

Just think how fast we will rebuild this country!

So I'm here to tell you that I know on first hand knowledge that the model and the necessity to have the Republic have its own monetary system, its' own banking system, are being worked on even as we speak.

We have to build our foundation by filling out everything that is required, and it starts with you, individually, building up the counties to strengthen them as the capacity of the Republic.

California is known to be the 8th largest economy in the world. Imagine that if all that economic capacity comes into the California Republic and we exclude the federal system of fraudulent taxation, and everything else that has been a parasite on us, imagine what strength and capacity California can be to lead the nation in leading the world.

Right here, right now, in this Jamboree tent, we have more capability to lead and change this world than anywhere else on the planet. Imagine that! All of you!!!

*Building Blocks of the Republic*

So I'm going to finish with one last concept. As I said, I've been studying history for 50 years. I've looked at how is it that we can be controlled, or have been controlled by a few men. There's a lot of lessons in law, and all of that, that I can't go into much detail now, but it does get down in law to one thing — CONSENT; by unknowing contract — by our contracting into a jurisdiction.

The word "jurisdiction" means an oath. "Juris" means law, but beneath it, it means an oath — a binding — by contract. So the **Declaration of Sovereign Rights** severs that contract of **presumption of attachment** from any foreign jurisdiction.

Your only jurisdiction, when you enter the Republic, is the Republic. Aside from that, in my exploration of history and law, and related things, I have boiled it down to understanding and seeing that there's been a continuum that goes back 5,000 years continuously in history, from Egypt, to Sumer, to Babylon, to Greece, all the way current. It's been a systematic, continuous agenda to arrive at this ENDPOINT where we're standing in time to be bound by contract, by oath of allegiance to a foreign power, to a system of eternal slavery for yourselves, your children, your grandchildren, and on down.

And believe me, we are at the sliver point of the precipice of that actually taking place! If we don't stand up and stop it right now, right here, it's gone forever. If you loose liberty, you loose it forever!

The control system boils down to two fundamental things; control of the laws, and control of the land.

We are controlled by the similitude of law, corporate rules known as codes, ordinances, statutes, and what have you, by an act of unknowing consent, by contract, by an oath of jurisdiction.

The land is another thing. We have been lifted off the land and put into a false reality of containment called equity.

Everything you know about title, and equity, and property, it's all part of the lie. It's now they manipulate the entire earth system, the money system, the tax system — you name it — because we are all dispossessed from the land.

The Republic has a means of establishing throughout the counties and the states at the national levels where we are establishing our own courts, our own local Grand Juries, where we are going to be able to sever that **presumption of attachment** in that false equity system and reclaim our land and bring the land into the Republic because you will hear the phrase, over and over again, as you study and learn about what the Republic is, which is the phrase, **"On the land."**

The land is the gift that we have been given from which and out of which all things come in terms of nourishment, the health, the wealth, the energy, the warmth, everything we need they have stolen it from us across the world, but they cannot hold onto it if we reclaim it. We have here in America mechanisms in law and foundations through the history of this country that no other people on this planet have.

We have the capacity — and it is being installed throughout the system in the Republic — for us to reclaim the land, because in the history of the world, only a Sovereign can hold the land. Everybody else is a serf or a slave. So learn what this means.

Understand the difference between the system you thought was real, and what it means to be on the land as a Sovereign in the Republic. A one-people-compact, one people, one nation under God.

Some day you'll be able to tell your grandchildren, "I helped to re-build, re-inhabit, and re establish the Republic that you now enjoy, in freedom, liberty, and justice for all.

*By buying a raffle ticket at a Jamboree!*

*[Audience Laughter]*

Thank you all. Enjoy the rest of your day!

## Re: Robert's Rules Of Order

One of the aspects of *Robert's Rules Of Order* for public meetings is this:

Under relaxed rules of procedure for general assemblies — such as committees, small boards and telecons — you may proceed with relaxed rules and only get formal when and if such a change becomes necessary.

Here are the relaxed rules available to committees, and such:

• You can make motions or speak without the necessity of formal recognition.

• Your motions do not have to be seconded.

• You can speak as often as you can politely obtain the attention of the other members. In fact, motions to *Limit Debate* are not in order.

• You can discuss things without a motion being on the floor.

• You don't have to take minutes in committees. However, having some record is useful, and it may be customary for your chairman to keep notes of committee proceedings for reference.

• Your chairman can make motions, participate in discussion, and vote.

This example may help:

We learned the relaxed rules of *Robert's Rules Of Order* in grammar school, even without knowing it. In class the teacher was the moderator, or chairman, if you prefer.

When we wished to "take the floor" to speak, we would raise our hand . . . and when recognized by the teacher . . . we were allowed to proceed. And when we were finished we would sit down.

In the case of a telecon, we might say, "I rise to speak" or simply, "May I speak?" And when recognized, proceed.

And when finished say, "I yield the floor."

What's more:

A vote can be taken by assuming a motion even where none has been formally made, and if it's abundantly clear that a particular decision is pending, that decision can be made by *unanimous consent*.

For example:

Suppose you've been talking about whether the fire truck you're recommending to the company commander should be a red fire truck or a white fire truck.

Your committee is sitting around the table, and you say, "The red fire truck is less expensive. Besides, the white one will show more dirt."

Bill says, "Yeah, I like red fire trucks better anyway."

The chairman then says, "Then I guess we will go with the red fire truck. Any objections?"

Without objections, you've just decided to buy a red fire truck or to at least recommend the purchase to your membership.

## CORPUS JURIS SECUNDUM
### SECTION 38A

§ 9 **De facto Grand Jury or Jurer**

There cannot be a grand jury de facto when there is a grand jury de jure.

It has been held that the **de facto officer doctrine** applies to an improperly appointed grand juror.

We're not called to fit in; we're called to stand out.

"God is well able to bring us into the land."

Republic for the united States of America
http://republicfortheunitedstates.org/

## Manual for the united States Republic
### An Introductory Review

# Policies, Procedures & Protocols
## Of The National Republic

## Other Publications

The Matrix As It Is: *A Different Point Of View*
http://tinyurl.com/6htky52

From Debt To Prosperity: *'Social Credit' Defined*
http://tinyurl.com/2vjgqay

Give Yourself Credit: *Money Doesn't Grow On Trees*
http://tinyurl.com/39eoywm

My Home Is My Castle: *Beware Of The Dog*
http://tinyurl.com/37wk48v

Commercial Redemption: *The Hidden Truth*
http://tinyurl.com/37tdbrf

Hardcore Redemption-In-Law: *Commercial Freedom And Release*
http://tinyurl.com/2ul4t5e

Oil Beneath Our Feet: *America's Energy Non-Crisis*
http://tinyurl.com/34dhbur

Untold History Of America: *Let The Truth Be Told*
http://tinyurl.com/36tkc9q

New Beginning Study Course: *Connect The Dots And See*
http://tinyurl.com/37n8cyj

Monitions of a Mountain Man: *Manna, Money, & Me*
http://tinyurl.com/377l66n

Maine Street Miracle: *Saving Yourself And America*
http://tinyurl.com/38lk966

Reclaim Your Sovereignty: *Take Back Your Christian Name*
http://tinyurl.com/392kzqr

Epistle to the Americans I: *What you don't know about The Income Tax*
http://tinyurl.com/3yz8mun

Epistle to the Americans II: *What you don't know about American History*
http://tinyurl.com/33cawzr

Epistle to the Americans III: *What you don't know about Money*
http://tinyurl.com/3az8r7w